The Bible Mystery And Meaning Of

The Teaching Of Jesus

Judge Thomas Troward

Kessinger Publishing's Rare Reprints

Thousands of Scarce and Hard-to-Find Books on These and other Subjects!

- Americana
- Ancient Mysteries
- Animals
- Anthropology
- Architecture
- Arts
- Astrology
- Bibliographies
- Biographies & Memoirs
- Body, Mind & Spirit
- Business & Investing
- Children & Young Adult
- Collectibles
- Comparative Religions
- Crafts & Hobbies
- Earth Sciences
- Education
- Ephemera
- Fiction
- Folklore
- Geography
- Health & Diet
- History
- Hobbies & Leisure
- Humor
- Illustrated Books
- Language & Culture
- Law
- Life Sciences
- Literature
- Medicine & Pharmacy
- Metaphysical
- Music
- Mystery & Crime
- Mythology
- Natural History
- Outdoor & Nature
- Philosophy
- Poetry
- Political Science
- Science
- Psychiatry & Psychology
- Reference
- Religion & Spiritualism
- Rhetoric
- Sacred Books
- Science Fiction
- Science & Technology
- Self-Help
- Social Sciences
- Symbolism
- Theatre & Drama
- Theology
- Travel & Explorations
- War & Military
- Women
- Yoga
- *Plus Much More!*

**We kindly invite you to view our catalog list at:
http://www.kessinger.net**

THIS ARTICLE WAS EXTRACTED FROM THE BOOK:

Bible Mystery and Bible Meaning

BY THIS AUTHOR:

Judge Thomas Troward

ISBN 0766100375

READ MORE ABOUT THE BOOK AT OUR WEB SITE:

http://www.kessinger.net

OR ORDER THE COMPLETE
BOOK FROM YOUR FAVORITE STORE

ISBN 0766100375

X.

THE TEACHING OF JESUS

IN this chapter I shall endeavor to give a connected idea of the general scope and purpose of the Master's teachings, the point of which we, in great measure, miss by taking particular sayings separately, and so losing the force which pertains to them, by reason of the place they hold in His system as a whole. For, be it remembered, Jesus was teaching a definite system, not a creed, nor a ritual, nor a code of speculative ethics, but a system resulting from the threefold source of spiritual inspiration, intellectual reasoning, and experimental observation, which are the three modes in which the Universal Mind manifests itself as Conscious Reasoning Power or "the Word." And therefore this system combines the religious, philosophical, and scientific characters, because it is a statement of the action of universal principles at the level where they find expression through the human mind.

As we proceed, we shall find that the basis of this system is the same perception of the unity between the Expressor and the Expressed, which is also the basis of the teaching of Moses, and which is summed up in the significant phrase I AM. Jesus brings out the consequences of this Unity in their relation to the Individual, and therefore presupposes the teaching of Moses, regarding the Universal Unity, as the necessary foundation for its reflection in the individual.

The great point to be noted, in the teaching of Jesus, is His statement of the absolute liberty of the individual. That was the subject of His first discourse in the synagogue of Nazareth (Luke iv. 16); He continued His teaching with the statement, "the truth shall make you free"; and He finished it with the final declaration before Pilate, that He had come into the world to the end that He should bear witness to the Truth (John xviii. 37). Thus, to teach us the knowledge of Liberating Truth was the beginning, the middle, and the end of the great work which the Master set before Him.

Now, there are two facts about this teaching that deserve our special attention. The first is that the perfect liberty of the individual must be in accordance with the will of God; for on any other supposition Jesus would have been teaching rebellion against the Divine will; and, therefore, any system of religion which inculcates blind submission to adverse circumstances, as submission to the will of God, must do so at the cost of branding Jesus as a leader of rebellion against the Divine authority.

The other point is that this freedom is represented simply as the result of coming *to know the Truth.* If words mean anything, this means that Liberty in truth exists at the present moment, and that what keeps us from enjoying it is simply our ignorance of the fact. In other words, the Master's teaching is that the essential, and, therefore, ever-present Law of each individual human life is absolute Liberty—it is so in the very nature of Being, and it is only our ingrained belief to the contrary that keeps us in bondage to all sorts of limitation.

Of course, it is easy to explain away all that the Master said, by interpreting it in the light of our past experiences; but these experiences themselves constitute the very bondage from which He came to deliver us, and, therefore, to do this is to destroy His whole work. We do not require His teaching to go back to the belittling and narrowing influence of past experiences; we do that naturally enough so long as we remain ignorant of any other possibilities. It is just this being tied up that we want to get loose from, and He came to tell us that, when we know the Truth, we shall find we are not tied up at all. If we hold fast to the initial teaching of Genesis, that the Divine Principle makes things by *itself becoming* them, then it follows that when it becomes the individual man, it cannot have any other than its own natural movement in him; that is, a continual pushing forward into fuller and fuller expression of itself, which, therefore, becomes fuller and fuller life in the individual; and, consequently, anything that tends to limit the full expression of the individual life must be abhorrent to the Universal Mind expressing itself *in that individuality*.

Then comes the question as to the way in which this truth is to be realized, and the practical way inculcated by the Master is very simple; it is only that we are to take this truth for granted, that is all. We may be ready to exclaim that this is a large demand upon our faith, but after all it is the only way in which we ever do anything. We take all the operations of the Life-principle in our physical body for granted, and what is wanted is a similar confidence in the working of our spiritual faculties.

We trust our bodily powers because we assume their action as the natural Law of our being; and in just the same way we can only use our interior powers, by tacitly assuming them to be as natural to us as any others. We must bear in mind that from first to last the Master's teaching was never other than a *veiled* statement of Truth: He spoke "the word" to the people in parables, and "without a parable spake He not unto them" (Matt. iv. 34). It is indeed added "and when they were alone He expounded all things to His disciples"; but if we take the interpretation of the parable of the sower as a sample, we can see how very far these expositions were from being a full and detailed explanation.

The thickest and outermost veil is removed, but we are still very far from that plain speaking among "the full-grown" which St. Paul tells us was equally distant from his own writing to the Corinthians. I say this on the best authority, that of the Master Himself. We might have supposed that in that last discourse, which commences with the fourteenth chapter of St. John's Gospel, He had withdrawn the final veil from His teaching; but, no, we have His own words for it that even this is a veiled statement of the Truth. He tells His disciples that the time when He shall show them plainly of "the Father" is still future (John xiv. 25).

He left the final interpretation to be given by the only possible interpreter, the Spirit of Truth, as the real significance of His words should in time dawn upon each of His hearers, with an inner meaning that would be none other than the revelation of The Sacred Name. As this meaning dawns upon us we find that Jesus no longer speaks to us in proverbs, but that His parables tell us plainly of "the Father," and our only wonder is that we did not discern His true meaning long ago.

He is telling us of great universal principles which are reproduced everywhere and in everything with special reference to their reproduction on the plane of Personality. He is not telling us of rules which God has laid down in one way, and could, had He chosen, have laid down in another, but of universal Laws which are the very Being of God, and which are, therefore, inherent in the constitution of Man. Let us, then, examine some of His sayings in this light.

The thread on which the pearls of the Master's teaching are strung together, is that Perfect Liberty is the natural result of knowing the Truth. "When you find what the Truth really is, you will find it to be that you are perfectly free," is the centre from which all His other statements radiate; but the final discovery cannot be made *for* you, you must each make it *for yourself*, therefore, "he that hath ears to hear let *him* hear."

This is nowhere brought out more clearly than in the parable of the Prodigal Son. The fact of sonship had never altered for either of the two brothers, but in different ways they each missed the point of their position as sons. The one limited himself by separating off a particular *share* of the Father's goods for himself, which, just because of being a limited share and not the whole, was speedily exhausted, leaving him in misery and want.

The other brother equally limited himself by supposing that he had no power to draw from his Father's stores, but must wait till he in some way acquired a specific permission to do so, not realizing his inherent right, as his Father's son, to take whatever he wanted.

The one son took up a false idea of independence, thinking it consisted in separating himself and, to use an expressive vulgarism, in being entirely "on his own hook," while the other, in his recoil from this conception, went to the opposite extreme, and believed himself to have no independence at all.

The younger son's return, so far from extinguishing the instinct of Liberty, gratified it to the full, by placing him in a position of honor and command in his Father's house; and the elder son is rebuked with the simple words, "Why wait for me to give you what is yours already? All that I have *is* thine." It would be impossible to state the relation between the Individual Mind and the Universal Mind more clearly than in this parable, or the two classes of error which prevent us from understanding and utilizing this relation.

The younger brother is the man who, not realizing his own spiritual nature, lives on the resources of the lower personality, till their failure to meet his needs drives him to look for something which cannot thus be exhausted, and eventually he finds it in the recognition of his own spiritual being as his inalienable birthright, because he was made in the image and likeness of God, and could not by any possibility have been created otherwise.

Gradually, as he becomes more and more conscious of the full effects of this recognition, he finds that "the Father" advances to meet him, until at last they are folded in each other's arms, and he realizes the true meaning of the words, "I and my Father are ONE." Then he learns that Liberty is in union and not in separation, and realizing his identity with the Infinite he finds that all its inexhaustible stores are open to him.

This is not rhapsody but simple fact, which becomes clear if we see that the only possible action of the undifferentiated Life-Principle must be to always press forward into fuller and fuller expression of itself, in particular forms of life, *in strict accordance with the conditions which each form provides for its manifestation.* And when any one thoroughly grasps this principle of the differentiation through form of an entirely undistributed universal potential, then he will see that the mode of differentiation depends on the direction in which the specializing entity is reaching out.

If he further gets some insight into the boundless possibilities which must result from this, he will realize the necessity, before all things, of seeking to reproduce in individuality that Harmonious Order which is the foundation of the universal system.

And, since he cannot particularize the whole Infinite at a single stroke, which would be a mathematical impossibility, he utilizes its boundless stores by particularizing, from moment to moment, the specific desires, powers, and attractions, which at that moment he requires to employ.

And, since the Energy from which he draws is infinite in quantity and unspecialized in quality, there is no limit either of extent or kind to the purposes for which he may employ it. But he can only do this by abiding in "the Father's" house, and by conforming to the rule of the house which is the Law of Love.

This is the only restriction, if it can be called a restriction to avoid using our powers injuriously; and this restriction becomes self-obvious, when we consider that the very thing which puts us in possession of this limitless power of drawing from the Infinite is the recognition of our identity with the Universal One, and that any employment of our powers to the intentional injury of others is in itself a direct denial of that "unity of the Spirit which is the bond of peace."

The binding power (religio) of Universal Love is thus seen to be inherent in the very nature of the Liberty, which we attain by the Knowledge of the Truth; but except this there is no other restriction. Why? Because, by the very hypothesis of the case, we are employing First Cause when we consciously use our creative power with the knowledge that our Thought is the *individual* action of the same Spirit which, in its universal action, is both the Cause and the Being of every mode of manifestation; for the great fact which distinguishes First Cause from secondary causation is its entire independence of all *conditions,* because it is not the outcome of conditions but itself creates them—it produces its own conditions step by step as it goes along.*

If, therefore, the Law of Love be taken as the foundation, *any* line of action can be worked out successfully and profitably; but this does not alter the fact that a higher degree of intelligence will see a much wider field of action than a lower one, and, therefore, if our field of activity is to grow, it can only be as the result of the growth of our intelligence; and, consequently, the first use we should make of our power of drawing from the Infinite should be for steady growth in understanding.

Life is the capacity for action and enjoyment, and, therefore, any extension of the field for the exercise of our capacities is an increase of our own livingness and enjoyment, and so the continual companionship of the Spirit of Truth, leading us into continually expanding perception of the limitless possibilities that are open to ourselves and to the whole race, is the supreme Vivifying Influence; and thus

---

*For fuller explanation regarding our use of First Cause, see my *Edinburgh Lectures on Mental Science.*

we find that the Spirit of Truth is identical with the Spirit of Life.

It is this consciousness of companionship that is the Presence of the Father; and it is in returning to this Presence and dwelling in it that we get back to the Source of our own spiritual nature, and so find ourselves in possession of boundless possibilities without any fear of misusing them, because we do not seek to be possessors of the Divine Power without being possessors of the Divine Love and Wisdom also.

And the elder brother is the man who has not thrown off the Divine guidance as the younger had done, but who has realized it only in the light of a restriction. Always his question is "Within what limits may I act?" and, consequently, starting with the idea of limitation, he finds limitation everywhere; and thus, though he does not go into a far country like his brother, he relegates himself to a position no better than that of a servant—his wages are measured by his work, his creeds, his orthodoxies, his limitations of all sorts and descriptions, which he imagines to be of Divine appointment, while all the time he has imported them himself.

But him also "the Father" meets with the gracious words, "Son, thou art *ever* with me, and all that I have *is* thine"; and, therefore, as soon as this elder brother becomes sufficiently enlightened to perceive that all the elements of restriction in his beliefs, save only the Law of Love, have no place in the ultimate reality of *Life,* he too re-enters the house, now no longer as a servant but as a son, and joins in the festival of everlasting joy.

We find the same lesson in the parable of the Talents. The use of the powers and opportunities we have, just where we are *now,* naturally opens up sequences by which still further opportunities, and, consequently, higher development of our powers become possible; and these higher developments in their turn open the way to yet further expansion, so that there is no limit to the process of growth other than what we set to it by denying or doubting the principle of growth in ourselves, which is what is meant by the servant burying his talent in the earth.

"The lord" is the Living Principle of Evolution which obtains equally on all planes, and nothing has been more fully established by science than the Law that as soon as progress stops retrogression begins, so that it is only by continual advance we can escape the penalty with which Professor Aytoun threatens us in his humorous verses, that we shall

"Return to the monad from which we all sprang,
  Which nobody can deny."

But on the other hand, the employment of our faculties and opportunities, so far as we realize them, is, by the same Law, certain to produce its own reward. By being faithful over a few things we shall become rulers over many things, for God is not unmindful to forget your labor of love, and so day by day we shall enter more and more fully into the joy of our Lord.

The same idea is repeated in the parable of the man who contrived to get into the wedding feast without the wedding garment. The Divine Marriage is the attainment by the individual mind of conscious union with the Universal Mind or "the Spirit"; and the feast, as in the parable of the Prodigal Son, signifies the joy which results from the attainment of Perfect Liberty, which means power over all the resources of the universe, whether within us or around us.

Now, as I have already pointed out, the only way in which this power can be used safely and profitably is through that recognition of its Source, which makes it in all points subservient to the Law of Love, and this was precisely what the intruder did not realize. He is the type of the man who fails in exactly the opposite way to the servant who buries his Lord's talent in the earth. This man has cultivated his powers to the uttermost, and so is able to enter along with the other guests. He has attained that Knowledge of the Laws of the spiritual side of Nature which gives him a place at that Table of the Lord, which is the storehouse of the Infinite; but he has missed the essential point of all his Knowledge, the recognition that the Law of Power is one with the Law of Love, and so, desiring to separate the Divine Power from the Divine Love, and to grasp the one while rejecting the other, he finds that the very Laws of which he has made himself master, by his knowledge, overwhelm him with their own tremendousness, and by their reflex action become the servants who bind him hand and foot, and cast him into the outer darkness. The Divine Power can never be separated with impunity from the Divine Love and Guidance.

The parable of the unjust steward is based upon the Law of the subjective nature of individual life. As in all the parables, "the lord" is the supreme Self-evolving Principle of the universe, which, relatively to us, is purely subjective, because it acts in and through ourselves. As such it follows the invariable Law of subjective mind, which is that of response to any suggestion that is impressed upon it with sufficient power.*

Consequently, "the lord" does not dispute the correctness of the accounts rendered by the steward, but, on the contrary, commends him for his wisdom in recognizing the true principle by which to escape the results of his past mal-administration of the estate.

---

*I have discussed tihs subject at greater length in my *Edinburgh Lectures on Mental Science*.

St. Paul tells us that he is truly approved "whom the Lord commendeth," and the commendation of the steward is unequivocally stated by Jesus, and, therefore, we must realize that we have here the statement of some principle which harmonizes with the Life-giving tendency of the Universal Spirit. And this principle is not far to seek. It is the acceptance by "the Lord" of less than the full amount due to Him.

It is the statement of Ezekiel xviii. 22, that if the wicked man forsake his way "he shall surely live and not die. All his transgressions that he hath committed shall not be mentioned unto him; in his righteousness that he hath done he shall live." It is what the Master speaks of as agreeing with the adversary while we are still in the way with him; in other words, it is the recognition that because the Laws of the universe are not vindictive but simply causal, therefore, the reversal of our former mis-employment of First Cause, which in our case is our Thought demonstrated in a particular line of action, must necessarily result in the reversal of all those evil consequences which would otherwise have flowed from our previous wrong-doing.

I have enlarged in a previous chapter on the operation of the Law of Suggestion with regard to the question of sacrifice; and when we either see that the Law of Sacrifice culminates in No Sacrifice, or reach the place where we realize that a Great and Sufficient Sacrifice has been offered up once for all, then we have that solid ground of suggestion which results in the summing-up of the whole Gospel in the simple words, "Don't do it again."

If we once realize the great truth stated in Psalm xviii. 26 and II. Samuel xxii. 27, that the Divine Universal Spirit always becomes to us exactly the correlative of our own principle of action, and that it does so naturally by the Law of Subjective Mind, then it must become clear that it can have no vindictive power in it, or, as the Bible expresses it, "Fury is not in Me" (Isaiah xxvii. 9).

But for the very same reason we canot trifle with the Great Mind by trying to impress one character upon it by our thought, while we are impressing another upon ourselves by our actions. This is to show our ignorance of the nature of the Law with which we are dealing; for a little consideration will show us that we cannot impress two opposite suggestions at the same time. The man who tried to do so is described in the parable of the servant, who threw his fellow-servant into prison after his own debt had been cancelled. The previous pardon availed him nothing, and he was cast into prison till he should pay the uttermost farthing.

The meaning becomes evident when we see that what we are dealing with is the supreme Law of our own being. We do not really believe what we do not act up to; if, therefore, we cast our fellow-servant into prison, no amount of philosophical speculation in an opposite direction will set us at liberty. Why? Because our action demonstrates that our real belief is in limitation. Such compulsion can only proceed from the idea that we shall be the poorer, if we do not screw the money out of our fellow-servant, and this is to deny our own power of drawing from the Infinite in the most emphatic manner, and so to destroy the whole edifice of Liberty.

We cannot impress upon ourselves too strongly the impossibility of living by two contradictory principles at the same time. And the same argument holds good when we conceive that the debt is due to our injured feelings, our pride, and the like—the principle is always the same; it is that perfect Liberty places us above the reach of all such considerations, because by the very hypothesis of being absolute freedom, it can create far more rapidly than any of our fellow-servants can run up debts; and our attitude towards those who are thus running up scores should be to endeavor to lead them into that region of fulness where the relation of debtor and creditor cannot exist, because it becomes merged in the radiation of creative power.

But perhaps the most impressive of all the parables was that in which, on the night when He was betrayed, the Master expressed the great mystery of God and Man by symbolic action rather than by words, girding Himself with a towel and washing the disciples' feet. He assured Peter that though the meaning of this symbolic act was not apparent at the time, it should become clear later on.

A wonderful light is thrown on this dramatization of a great principle by comparing it with the Master's utterance in Luke xiii. 35-37. The idea of girding is very conspicuous in that parable. First, we are bidden to have our loins girded and our lights burning, like unto men that wait for their Lord. Then we are told that, if the servants are found thus prepared, when the Lord does come *the positions will be reversed*, and He will make *them* sit down and will gird Himself and serve *them*.

Now, what Jesus in this parable taught in words, He taught on the night of the Last Supper in acts. There is a strict parallel; in both cases the Master, the Lord, girds Himself and serves those who had hitherto accounted themselves His servants. The emphatic reduplication of this parable shows that here we have something of the very highest importance presented to us; and, undoubtedly, it is the veiled statement of the supreme mystery of individual being. And this mystery is the raising to the highest spiritual levels of the old maxim that Nature will obey us in proportion as we first obey Nature. This is the ordinary rule of all science. The universal principles can never act contrary to themselves, whether on the spiritual or the physical level, and, therefore, unless we are prepared by study of the Law and obedience to it, we cannot make use of these principles at any level; but granted such preparation on our part, and the Law becomes our humble servant, obeying us in every particular on the one condition that we first obey it.

It is thus that modern science has made us masters of a world of power which, for all practical purposes, did not exist in the times of the Tudors; and, transferring this truth to the highest and innermost, to the very Principle of Life itself, the meaning becomes plain. Because the Life-Principle is not something separate from ourselves, but is the Supporter of our individuality, therefore, the more we understand and obey its great *generic* Law, the more fully shall we be able to make any *specific* applications of it that we like. But on one condition. We must be washed. "If I wash thee not thou hast no part with Me," were the words of the Master. He spoke as the conscious mouthpiece of the Universal Spirit, and this must, therefore, be taken as the personal utterance of the Spirit itself; and seen in this light the meaning becomes clear; we must first be cleansed by the Spirit.

And here we meet with another symbolical fact of the highest importance. This dramatization of the final truth of spiritual knowledge took place after the supper was ended. Now, as we all know, the supper was itself of supreme symbolical significance. It was the Jewish Passover and the Christian Commemoration, and tradition tells us it was also the symbolic act by which, throughout antiquity, the highest initiates signified their identical realization of Truth, however apparently separated by outward forms or nationality.

We find these mystical emblems of bread and wine presented to Abraham by Melchizedek, himself the type of the man who has realized the supreme truth of the birth which is "without father, without mother, without beginning of days or end of years"; and, therefore, if we would grasp the full meaning of the Master's action on that last night, we must understand the meaning of the symbolic meal of which He and His followers had just partaken. Briefly stated, it is the recognition by the participant of his unity with, and power of appropriating, the Divine in its twofold mode of Spirit and Substance.

Science and Religion are not two separate things. They both have the same object, to bring us nearer and nearer to the point where we shall find ourselves in touch with the ONE Universal Cause. Therefore, the two were never dissociated by the greatest thinkers of antiquity, and the inseparableness of energy and matter, which is now recognized by the most advanced science as the starting-point of all its speculations, is none other than the old, old doctrine of the identity of Spirit and ultimate Substance.

Now, it is this twofold nature of the Universal First Cause that is symbolized by bread and wine. The fluid and the solid, or Spirit and Substance, as the two universal supports of all manifested Forms—these are the universal principles which the two typical elements signify. But in order that the individual may be consciously benefited by them, he must recognize his own participation in them, and he denotes his Knowledge on this point by eating the bread and drinking the wine; and his intention in so doing is to signify his recognition of two great facts; one, that he lives by continually drawing from the Infinite Spirit in its twofold unity; and the other, that he not only does this automatically, but also has power to consciously differentiate the Universal Energy for any specific purpose that he will.

Now, this combination of dependence and control could not be more perfectly symbolized than by the acts of eating and drinking—we cannot do without food, but it is at our own discretion to select what and when we shall eat. And if we realize the true meaning of "the Christ," we shall see that it is that principle of Perfected Humanity which is the highest expression of the Universal Spirit-Substance; and taken in this sense, the bread and wine are fitting emblems of the flesh and blood, or Substance and

Spirit, of "the Son of Man," the ideal Type of all Humanity.

And so it is that we cannot realize the Eternal Life except by consciously partaking of the innermost Life-Principle, with due recognition of its true nature—not meaning the mere observance of a ceremonial rite, however august in its associations, and however useful as a powerful suggestion; but meaning personal recognition of the Supreme Truth which that rite signifies.

This, then, was the meaning of the symbolic meal which had just concluded. It indicated the participant's recognition of his union with the Universal Spirit, as being the supreme fact on which his individual life was based, the ultimate of all Truth. Now, the word rendered "washed," in John xiii. 10, is more correctly given in the Revised Version as "bathed," a word which signifies total immersion. But no "bathing" had taken place on this occasion; to what, then, did Jesus allude when He spoke to His disciples as men who had been "bathed"? It is precisely that which, in Ephesians v. 26, is spoken of as "the washing of water by the word"; "water" being, as we have already seen, the Universal Substance, and "the word" the synonym for that Intelligence which is the very essence of Spirit. The meaning, then, is that by partaking of this symbolic meal they had signified their recognition of their own total immersion in the ONE Universal Divine Being, which is at once both

Spirit and Substance; and since they could not conceive of It otherwise than as Most Holy, this recognition must thenceforward have a purifying influence upon the whole man.

This great recognition does not need to be repeated—seen once it is seen for ever; and, therefore, "he that is washed needeth not save to wash his feet, but is clean every whit." But though the principle is grasped—which, of course, is the substantial foundation of the new life—immediate perfection does not follow. Very far from it. And so we have to come day by day to the Spirit, for the washing away of those stains which we contract in our daily walk through life. "If we say that we have no sin, the truth is not in us; but if we confess our sin, He is faithful and just to forgive us our sin and to cleanse us from all unrighteousness."

It is this daily confession, not to man, but to the Divine Spirit Itself, which produces the daily cleansing, and thus Its first service to us is to wash our feet. If we thus receive the daily washing, we shall, day by day, put away from us that sense of separation from the Divine Universal Mind, which only the conscious retention of guilt in the heart can produce, after once we have been "bathed" by the recognition of our individual relation to It; and if our study of the Bible has taught us anything, it has taught us that the very Essence of Life is in its identity and unity throughout all forms of manifestation.

To allow ourselves, therefore, to remain conscious of separation from the Spirit of the Whole is to accept the idea of Disintegration, which is the very principle of death; and if we thus accept death at the fountain-head, it must necessarily spread through the whole stream of our individual existence and poison the waters. But it is inconceivable that any one who has once realized the Great Unity, should ever again willingly remain in conscious separation from it, and, therefore, immediate open-hearted approach to the Divine Spirit is the ever ready remedy as soon as any consciousness of separation makes itself felt.

And the symbol includes yet another meaning. If the bathing or total immersion signifies our unity with the Spirit of the Whole, then the washing of the feet must signify the same thing in a lesser degree, and the meaning implied is the ever-present attendance of the Infinite Undifferentiated Spirit ready to be differentiated by us to any daily service, no matter how lowly. Seen in this light, this acted parable is not a mere reminder of our imperfection, which, unless corrected by a sense of power, could only be a perpetual suggestion of weakness that would incapacitate us from doing anything; but it indicates our continual command over all the resources of the Infinite, for every object that all the endless succession of days can ever bring before us. We may draw from it what we like, when we like, and for what purpose we like; nothing can prevent us but ignorance or consciousness of separation.

The idea thus graphically set forth, was expanded throughout that marvellous discourse with which the Master's ministry in His mortal body terminated. As ever, His theme was the perfect Liberty of the individual resulting from recognition of our true relation to the Universal Mind. The ONE great I AM is the Vine, the lesser ones are the branches. We cannot bear fruit except we abide in the Vine; but abiding in it there is no limit to the developments we may attain.

The Spirit of Truth will guide us into *all* Truth, and the possession of all Truth must carry the possession of all Power along with it; and since the Spirit of Truth can be none other than the Spirit of Life, to be guided into all Truth must be to be guided into the Power of an endless life.

This does not need our removal from the world: "I pray not that Thou shouldest take them out of the world, but that Thou shouldest keep them from the evil." What is needed is ceasing to eat of that poisonous fruit, the tasting of which expelled Man from the Paradise he is designed to inhabit. The true recognition of the ONE leaves no place for any other; and if we follow the Master's direction not to estimate things by their superficial appearance, but by their central principle of being, then we shall find that nothing is evil in essence, and that the origin of evil is always in a wrong application of what is good in itself, thus bringing us back to the declaration of the first chapter of Genesis, that God saw all that He had created, "and behold it was very good."

If, then, we realize that our Liberty resides in the creative power of our Thought, we shall see the immense importance of recognizing the essence of things as distinguished from the misplaced order in which we often first become acquainted with them. If we let our Thought dwell on an inverted order we perpetuate that order; but if, going below the surface, we fix our Thought upon the essential nature of things, and see that it is logically impossible for anything to be *essentially* bad which is a specific expression of the Universal Good, then we shall in our Thought call all things good, and so help to bring about that golden age when the old inverted order shall have passed away, and a new world of joy and liberty shall take its place.

This, then, is briefly the line followed by the Master's teaching, and His miracles were simply the natural outcome of His perfect recognition of His own principles. Already the unfolding recognition of these principles is beginning to produce the same results at the present day, and the number of well-authenticated cures effected by mental means increases every year. And this is precisely in accordance with Jesus' own prediction. He enumerated the signs which should follow those who really believed what He really taught, and in so saying He was simply making a statement of cause and effect. He never set up His power as proof of a nature different from our own; on the contrary, He said that those who learned what He taught should eventually be able to do still greater miracles, and He summed up the whole position in the words, "the disciple when he is perfected shall be as his Master."

Again, He laid special stress on the perfect naturalness of all that He taught, by guarding us against the error of supposing that the intervention of any intermediary was required between us and "the Father." If we could assign such a position to any being it would be to Himself, but He emphatically disclaims it. "In that day ye shall ask in My name; *and I say not unto you that I will pray the Father for you,* for the Father Himself loveth you, because ye have loved Me and believed that I came forth from the Father" (John xvi. 26). If the student has realized what has been said in the chapter on "the Sacred Name," he will see that the opening words of this utterance can be nothing else than a statement of universal Truth; and that the love and belief in Himself, spoken of in the concluding clause, are the love of this Truth exhibited in its highest form as Man evolved to perfection, and belief in the power of the Spirit to produce such an evolution.

I do not say that there is nothing personal in the statement; on the contrary, it is eminently personal to "the Man Christ Jesus," but as the Type of Perfected Humanity—the first-fruit of the further evolution which is to complete the pyramid of manifested being upon earth by the introduction of the Fifth Kingdom, which is that of the Spirit.

When we realize what is accomplished in Him, we see what is potential in ourselves; and since we have now reached the point beyond which any further evolution can only result from our conscious co-operation with the evolutionary principle, all our future progress depends on the extent to which we do recognize the potentialities contained in our own individuality.

Therefore, to realize the manifestation of the Divine which Jesus stands for, and to love it, is the indispensable condition for attaining that access to "the Father" which means the full development in ourselves of all the powers of the Spirit.

The point which rivets our attention in this utterance of the Master's is the fact that we do not need the intervention of any third party to beseech "the Father" for us, because "the Father" Himself loves us. This statement, which we may well call the greatest of all the teachings of Jesus, setting us free, as it does, from the cramping influences of a limited and imperfect theology, He has bracketed together with the recognition of Himself; and therefore, if we would follow His teaching, we cannot separate these two things which He has joined; but if we realize in Him the embodiment of the Divine Ideal of Humanity, His meaning becomes clear—it is that our recognition of this ideal is itself the very thing that places us in immediate touch with "the Father."

By accepting the Divine Ideal as our own, we *provide the conditions* under which the Undifferentiated Universal Subconscious Mind becomes able to differentiate Itself into the particular and concrete expression of that Potential of Personality which is eternally inherent in It; and thus, in each one who realizes the Truth which the Master taught, the Universal Mind attains an individualization capable of consciously recognizing Itself.

To attain this is the great end of Evolution, and in thus gaining Its end the ONE becomes the MANY, and the MANY return into the ONE; not by an absorption depriving them of individual identity, which would be to stultify the entire operation of the Spirit in Evolution by simply ending where it had begun, but by impressing upon innumerable individualities the perfect and completed likeness of that

Original in the *potential* image of which they were first created.

The entire Bible is the unfolding of its initial statement that Man is made in the image of God, and the teaching of Jesus is the proclamation and demonstration of this Truth in its complete development, the Individual rejoicing in perfect Life and Liberty because of his conscious ONE-ness with the Universal.

The teaching of Jesus, whether by word or deed, may, therefore, be summed up as follows. He says in effect to each of us: What you really are in essence is a concentration of the ONE Universal Life-Spirit into conscious Individuality—if you live from the recognition of this Truth as your starting-point, it makes you Free. You cannot do this so long as you imagine that you have one centre and the Infinite another—you can only do it by recognizing that the two centres coincide, and that That which, as being Infinite, is incapable of centralization in Itself, finds centre in you.

Think of these things until you see that it is impossible for them to be otherwise, and then step forward in perfect confidence, knowing that the universal principles must necessarily act with the same mathematical precision in yourself, that they do in the attractions of matter or in the vibrations of ether. His teaching is identical with the teaching of Moses, that there is only ONE Being anywhere, and that the various degrees of its manifested consciousness are to be measured by one standard—the recognition of the meaning of the words I AM.

I have endeavored to show that the Bible is neither a collection of traditions belonging only to a petty tribe, nor yet a statement of dogmas which can give no account of themselves beyond the protestation that they are mysteries which must be accepted by faith —which faith, when we come to analyze it, consists only in accepting the bare assertion of those very persons who, when we ask them for the explanation of the things they bid us believe, are unable to give any explanation beyond the word "MYSTERY."

The true element of Mystery we shall never get rid of, for it is inherent in the ultimate nature of all things; but it is an element that perpetually unfolds, inviting us at each step to still further inquiry by satisfactorily and intelligently answering every question that we put in really logical succession, and thus the Mystery continually opens out into Meaning and never pulls us up short with an anathema for our irreverence in daring to inquire into Divine secrets.

When the interrogated is driven to the fulmination of anathemas, it is very plain that he has reached the end of his tether. As Byran says in "Don Juan"—

"He knew not what to say, and so he swore";

and therefore this mode of answering a question

always indicates one of two things, ignorance of the subject or intentional concealment of facts, and on either alternative, any "authority" which thus only tells us to "shut up" thereby at once loses all claim to our regard. Every undiscovered fact in the great Universal Order is a Divine Secret until we find the key that unlocks it; but the Psalmist tells us that the secret of the Lord is with them that fear Him, and the Master says that there is nothing hidden that shall not be revealed.

To seek, therefore, to understand the great principles on which it is written, so far from being an act of presumption, is the most practical proof we can give of our reverence for the Sacred Volume; and if the foregoing pages have in any way helped the reader to see in the Bible a statement of the working of Laws, which are inherent in the nature of things and follow an intelligible sequence of cause and effect, my purpose in writing will be answered.

The limited space at my disposal has allowed me only to treat the whole subject in an introductory manner, and in particular I have not yet shown the method by which the ONE Universal Principle follows out an *exclusive* line of unfoldment, building up a "Chosen People" by a process of *natural selection* culminating in the Great Central Figure of the Gospels. It does this without in any way departing from its *universal* character, for it is that Power which cannot deny itself; but it does it as a consequence of this very universality, and upon the importance of this specialized action of the Universal Principle to the future development of the race, it is impossible to lay too much stress.

The Bible tells us that there is such a special selection, and if we have found truth in its more general statements, we may reasonably expect to find the same truth in its more specialized statements also.

This is the end of this publication.

Any remaining blank pages are for our book binding requirements and are blank on purpose.

To search thousands of interesting publications like this one, please remember to visit our website at:

http://www.kessinger.net

CPSIA information can be obtained
at www.ICGtesting.com
Printed in the USA
LVOW09s0016260318
571140LV00003B/31/P